# SERVANTHOOD AS WORSHIP

*The Privilege of Life in a Local Church*

**Nate Palmer**
Cruciform Press | Released December, 2010

To my wife, Steph, who through her example has taught me more about service than anyone else. To my friend Toby Kurth, your encouragement and help was invaulable. To Emily James, your writing expertise made a huge impact. To the Pastors and members of Grace Church Frisco who model Christian service every day.
-Nate Palmer

CruciformPress

"In an age where the church can be likened to Cinderella—beautiful, but largely ignored and forgotten—Nate Palmer's book forces us to rethink both the church and our relationship to her. In an age where egocentrism ensures that we sing, 'O say, can you see—what's in it for me?' on a weekly basis, Palmer forces us to say instead, 'How can I best serve the church?'

Looking at the needs of others rather than one's own is possibly the most serious deficiency in the church today. Reading this book will help redress the deficiency. I heartily recommend it."

**Derek W. H. Thomas**, John E. Richards Professor of Theology, Reformed Theological Seminary (Jackson); Minister of Teaching, First Presbyterian Church, Jackson, MS

"Think of these pages as a handbook. Put this handbook into the hands of your people and you will give them a sustainable, practical vision for serving in the local church that is powered by grace. Along the way, they will also pick up a mini theological education"

**Justin Buzzard**, pastor, San Francisco Bay Area; author, BuzzardBlog.com

"In our media-crazed, me-first culture, the art of the basin and the towel has been shoved off onto those who get paid to serve—certainly a call to serve in humility can't be God's will for all of us, or could it?

In this helpful book, Nate Palmer gets at the heart of our resistance and portrays our dear Savior's humiliation in his acts of service for us—not only as our example but also as our righteousness. I strongly recommend this book."

**Elyse Fitzpatrick**, author of *Because He Loves Me*

# Table of Contents

CruciformPress.com

Published by Cruciform Press, Adelphi, Maryland | info@CruciformPress.com |
Copyright © 2010 by Nathan Palmer, All rights reserved. | ISBN: 978-1-4538187-7-0
| Unless otherwise indicated, all Scripture quotations are taken from: The Holy Bible:
English Standard Version, Copyright © 2001 by Crossway Bibles, a division of Good
News Publishers. Used by permission. All rights reserved. | Italics or bold text within
Scripture quotations indicate emphasis added.

# One
# **SERVICE**

### The Ministry of All Believers

"Can you serve in the nursery this morning?" As you try to pick one of the more plausible excuses that have popped into your head, you secretly hope the pastor's question was theoretical. You know you should say, "Sure, I will serve anywhere!" but you just can't. The last place you want to be is with a bunch of screaming babies, having to change diapers and dodge spit-ups while your friends enjoy the sermon. Why you? Can't someone else do it?

You're awakened by an obnoxious alarm clock. It's 5:30 Sunday morning, and outside the rain is coming down in sheets. You must get up, but you don't want to. *This is what, the third week in a row?* The thought of once again going to help set up the auditorium in the school where your church meets is paralyzing. Picking up the van, hauling the equipment into the building in the rain—you'll need to bring extra clothes. You wonder if it is possible to catch the flu before it's time to leave. Why you? Can't someone else do it?

If these situations are at all familiar, I know how you feel. When I became a Christian at age twenty-five, I was so happy and energized by the wonder of my salvation that I didn't mind serving on Sunday mornings. I enjoyed it. It seemed only natural that, as a new member, I would help with the chores. Doing odd jobs before church seemed like a way to pay for all the joy and benefit I was receiving. Plus, as part of a new church plant that met in a school, there were far more tasks than there were people to do them. Someone had to serve or we couldn't "have" church. And so, week after week, I did my duty.

During those early months of my Christian walk, however, serving gradually became a mixed bag of emotions and competing motivations. What started out as a way to express my joy soon became, in my mind, a way to manage God. My service was like the volume knob on a car stereo—I could amplify God's opinion of me by serving more. If I'd had a bad week, frequently giving in to temptation or not reading the Bible, I would just go to church early and serve. In my mind, the exchange rate was something like one act of service for one sin. *God will have to like me again once he sees how hard I'm trying to make up for my failures.* This form of atoning for sin was easier than actually facing my problems and trying to work on them.

After a few short months I had completely flipped salvation upside down. I was managing God and serving myself instead of managing my responsibilities and serving God. I had rewritten the rule book to put myself in charge. I had exchanged Christ's service on the cross for the merit of my serving in the church.

As serving became a tedious process of self-justification, it took a toll on my affections for God and the church. It became harder and harder to show up. Hooking up audio cables became pure monotony. Every Sunday I would do the same thing and nobody ever thanked me or acknowledged my effort. No one seemed to care that I got up insanely early to haul heavy stuff around, only to have to change out of my completely sweaty shirt. Everyone else enjoyed their weekends while I toiled. It didn't seem fair. I actually began to dread Sundays. The whole concept of serving became thankless and meaningless, a colossal waste of time and — let's not forget — talent. I constantly asked myself, *Why me? Can't someone else do it?*

It was at this point in my life that I became addicted to a drug: leadership. I saw that maybe there really was an upside to serving. *Eventually the church leaders will notice, right? Isn't it those who are faithful in the small things who are given greater responsibilities?* Servanthood took on a useful new

role — a springboard to leadership in the church —
and mysteriously my vigor for serving returned.
Sure, I was subtle about it, but now all those audio
cables were a means to a new end. Once you're
already using your serving (you imagine) to manage
God, how much easier is it to manipulate men? As
I served to gain attention, the church leadership
would see my works and place me in some important
position. Serving as a vehicle to advance my personal
ambitions? Let it rain!

In a few short months, my attitude toward
serving had gone from thrilled to ambivalent to
resentful to selfishly ambitious. Why the roller
coaster ride? Largely because I had no clear idea
what the Bible teaches about serving. I didn't know,
from God's perspective, why I was doing it. So I did
it for my own reasons.

I know that some churches have essentially zero
expectations that members will pitch in to help.
Other churches have enough resources that there
is little or no need for the average member to serve
in practical ways. But a great many churches follow
the biblical model, which values servanthood in
itself. Are you in a church like that? Then at some
point you will definitely struggle with serving. You
probably have already. Service, of course, can come
in many forms — building maintenance, children's
ministry, worship music, local outreach, tech

support, missions trips, and a hundred others. But if you don't really know why you are called to serve in the church of Jesus Christ, your attitude will be as unstable and unhealthy as mine was.

In this book, I want to provide the theological framework that Christians need to understand what serving in the local church is really all about. When we are informed by a biblical understanding of service, it changes everything.

The first thing we need to see is that service is inescapable. Literally.

## Full-Time Servants

Do you realize that serving is a constant activity? It's like breathing. There is never a moment when we are not serving someone. None of us are ever on the sidelines, waiting to get into the game of servanthood. Since birth, every one of us has been actively serving.

Most of the time we are simply serving ourselves—pouring our energy and hope for happiness into the nurture of our own desires. But at each moment, we are serving either the desires of our flesh or the desires of God. As Paul Tripp states, "Each of our lives is shaped by the war between the kingdom of God and the kingdom of self."[1]

The conflict is that we don't want to be subservient to anyone else's wants and needs. Not even God's. This poses a problem, as Jesus points out, for we cannot obey both God and our own interests at the same time: "No one can serve two masters, for either he will hate the one and love the other, or he will be devoted to the one and despise the other" (Matthew 6:24). Either we labor for God or for an entirely different master. This isn't always the kind of servanthood I want to embrace. Often I prefer my own kingdom—the one where I am the object of worship and I get to define servanthood (usually as me serving me and others serving me). We always serve who we see as the king of our kingdom. That's why servanthood and worship are essentially the same thing.

But biblical service requires that we prefer others over ourselves, that we sacrifice willingly, giving time and energy that could have been used for personal benefit to benefit others. Biblical service calls us to direct our focus outward. In this we imitate Christ, who served others to the point of death. As I will emphasize throughout this book, serving God as a grateful response to the gospel is the calling of every Christian.

## The Vision and the Need

All healthy churches, regardless of size or resources, seek to integrate their members into the life of the church through service. These churches see servanthood as both biblical and essential to church life. There are a *lot* of established evangelical churches that take this view, and new ones are started every day. Approximately 4,000 churches are planted each year in the United States alone.[2]Many of these new churches are started through networks like Acts 29, which saw overall attendance double in 2009 while planting fifty-five churches.[3]

Regardless of a church's age or size, a biblical vision for serving is vital to building a healthy church. Who are the servants in a particular church actually serving? What are their motivations? Are they more interested in serving God's purposes or their own? Many churches succeed or fail on the answers to such questions.

Given the number of existing churches, plus the explosive growth in the creation of new churches, there is a huge need for people to serve, and serve for the right reasons. Pastor and author John Stott wonders when Christians will recover "the ministry of all believers"[4] in which each Christian exercises his or her gifts in ministry to others.

Serving in the church is not just the privilege of the few. It is the call of every Christian's life. (The Appendix addresses this subject more thoroughly, although I suggest you read it later.) Paul writes, "There is one body and one Spirit—just as you were called to the one hope that belongs to your call—one Lord, one faith, one baptism, one God and

Father of all, who is over all and through all and in all. But grace was given to each one of us according to the measure of Christ's gift" (Ephesians 4:4-7). While roles may be formal or informal, creative or mundane, physical or intellectual, the goal is the same: to glorify God and magnify the gospel to the benefit of others.

Each of us has been given gifts, and each of us are called to use our gifts as a light before men. When biblical, gospel-centered service in Christ's name is present at the center of a local church, it forms a brilliant nucleus radiating out into a dark world. This brilliance is something the church must recover. That recovery starts with a theological foundation of servanthood. The purpose of this book is to present a biblical vision of service so that believers from all sorts of churches can say, along with Joshua, "But as for me and my house, we will serve the Lord" (Joshua 24:15).

Two
# LINEAGE

Service Began with God in Christ

In the mid-1700s, Linville Creek Baptist
Church was at the vanguard of English colonialism
in Virginia. The church was frequently attacked by
the local Native American tribes, but on September
21, 1757, the little frontier church was harassed by
a different kind of assailant. Reverend Alexander
Miller and some of his followers from a nearby
Presbyterian church interrupted a service, insulted
the preacher by calling him a papist, and took over
the pulpit. Reverend Miller then proceeded to
lecture the entire Baptist congregation on the merits
of infant baptism.

When my father retired from work a few years
back, he started researching our family's history.
Our genealogical tree contains missionaries,
nobles, criminals, war veterans, frontier scouts,
and businessmen. Among these ancestors is the
presumptuous Reverend Miller. I'm sure he never

dreamed that, centuries later, his descendants would be able to uncover this story and, when they did, would scratch their heads and say, "What in the world was he thinking?" Yet if there had been no Alexander Miller, I would not have been born. My children and I are his legacy, and he is our lineage.

Recently I was reminiscing over my testimony with some friends, one of whom God had used to first illuminate the gospel to me. He pointed out that if it hadn't been for the person who shared the gospel with him, he would not have been equipped to help me. I began to wonder—if I charted that line of serving from person to person, what wonderful stories of God's faithfulness and love might I find? I soon realized that, whatever the intricate and wonderful details along the way, my spiritual lineage actually goes back in a direct line to Jesus Christ.

My spiritual family tree—just like yours—is filled with people who responded to the gospel by modeling Christ's love and service to others. But holding the first position in that tree is the One who started it all, Jesus Christ. Every genealogy of biblical service finds its source at the same place: the ultimate service of the Son of God dying in the place of sinners, that they may spend eternity with God in Heaven. On the cross, Jesus cleansed the sin of all believers for all time. His gospel has flowed from one generation to another for 2,000 years by the Spirit-empowered, grace-empowered service of one sinner to another.

Will you and I keep it going? Or will it end here? How can we help ensure that the waterfall of grace will continue flowing to future generations?

It all begins with our theological understanding. Motive and intention, derived from our spiritual lineage in Christ, are what distinguish Christian service from worldly service.

## The Roots of Christian Service

To begin with the most important point, and the most easily forgotten, we do not serve to earn God's love or favor. As Christians, our standing with God — our very salvation — does not depend on whether we serve, but that Christ first served us. "We love because he first loved us" (1 John 4:19). All our service *for* God begins and ends with service *from* God. God created us, God sustained us despite our sin, and God saved us from our sin. Christ's service did not begin with the incarnation. It started at creation, continues today through his exaltation, and will include his second coming and eternity in his presence.

**Creation.** John's first epistle tells us we were created through Christ from the beginning of the universe. Likewise, Paul writes that we were chosen in Christ before the foundation of the world (Ephesians 1:4).

Man and woman were created in God's image not just in form, but also in purity. Then something terrible happened: Adam disobeyed God by eating the forbidden fruit and sin entered the world (Genesis 3). The effect of man's sin was devastating and comprehensive, so much so that Adam's descendants inherited his fallen nature. Man could no longer serve like he was created to do. Every human has therefore not only sinned in Adam but, as Paul explains in Romans 3:9-19, every person has individually sinned. Everyone falls short of the perfect standard God requires.

**Sustaining.** Once Adam and Eve sinned, one thing was certain: humanity would be an entire race of failures and rebels. God could have easily and in perfect justice cut the whole thing short and destroyed mankind. But he didn't. Instead he made a promise of salvation, right there in the Garden (Genesis 3:14-15). When we couldn't help ourselves out of our dire predicament, God decided to do it for us. When our fate was sealed and we were without hope, God decided to change our fate. He chose to serve us, and he communicated that choice through a promise. The rest of human history is the story of how God's promise was, is, and will be fulfilled through God's unendingly faithful service to us.

Generations after Eden, when it was necessary to purge the earth of runaway sin, God kept his

promise by leaving a remnant in Noah. God later
elaborated on the promise, unfolding it a little at
a time as he spoke to Abraham, to Moses, and to
others such as Isaiah (Isaiah 53), Daniel (Daniel 7),
Jeremiah (Jeremiah 32), and more. At every point,
God served mankind not only by withholding his
judgment, but by directing events toward the day
when Christ would come.

**Incarnation.** In the Person of Christ, God
continued his service to us in the incarnation. He
humbled himself by taking the likeness of a man
so that we may, as Paul explains in Galatians 4:5,
"receive adoption as sons." Christ's humiliation is for
our benefit: Jesus came, not because man had finally
obtained perfection, but because we never could.

**Death.** Jesus then served us in the most extreme
possible way, not only dying the physical death we
deserved, but enduring the wrath of God as payment
for our sins. "God shows his love for us in that while
we were still sinners, Christ died for us" (Romans
5:8). There is no service we could ever perform for
anyone, God or man, that would equal a fraction
of the service Jesus rendered to us at the cross. How
marvelous, then, that God does not demand this of
us, for all such work is finished! (John 19:30)

**Resurrection, Ascension, Exaltation.** Yet
Christ's atoning sacrifice, for all its drama and
uniqueness, was not the end of God's service to

17

man. It was the beginning of an entirely new form of service, for three days after Jesus' death, he was resurrected. He spent forty days ministering to his followers, and then ascended into Heaven and sat down at the right hand of God the Father (Mark 16:19). As Paul explains, "[God] worked in Christ when he raised him from the dead and seated him at his right hand in the heavenly places, far above all rule and authority and power and dominion, and above every name that is named, not only in this age but also in the one to come" (Ephesians 1:20-21).

Thomas Watson puts it aptly when he writes, "In his humiliation he descended so low, that it was not fit to go lower; and in his exaltation he ascended so high that it is not possible to go higher."[5] John Calvin explains that the phrase *right hand of God* means, "that Christ was invested with lordship over heaven and earth, and solemnly entered possession of the government committed to him."[6]

In Christ's exaltation, God gave Jesus the power and authority to rule over everything, and in everything rule perfectly. Jesus was given this position so that he could properly fulfill the supreme governmental office to which he ascended. This government of Christ is made up of three distinct roles that he uniquely fulfills: Prophet, Priest, and King. The Westminster Shorter Catechism (which I'm paraphrasing) defines each of the roles.

- As Prophet, Christ reveals the will of God to us for our salvation by his Word and Spirit.
- As Priest, Christ offered himself up once as a sacrifice for us to satisfy divine justice and to reconcile us to God, and he continually intercedes for us.
- As King, Christ brings us under his power, rules and defends us, and restrains and conquers all his and all our enemies.[7]

Christ continues to serve mankind from heaven by fulfilling each of these positions, simultaneously and perfectly.

Perhaps the most important aspect of Christ's exaltation was that it made possible the sending of the Holy Spirit. Christ clearly explained to his disciples that it was for their benefit that he should be taken into Heaven. Only after his ascension and exaltation was it possible for the Holy Spirit to be sent as their Helper—and ours.

This sending of the Holy Spirit is done as part of Christ's intercession on our behalf. It is common among Christians to think of intercession as involving only one thing—Jesus coming before the Father, proclaiming that our sin has been paid for. But the definition is broader than this. Louis Berkhof explains, "Christ's ministry of intercession is also a ministry of loving care for his people. He helps them in their difficulties, their trials, and their temptations."[8] This form of intercession involves Jesus sending us the Holy Spirit.

The Spirit works within us to magnify Christ, piercing the veil of sin and helping us comprehend the things of God. He enlightens the meaning of Scripture and convicts our conscience of the sins we commit. Without the Holy Spirit, we could not even understand the gospel (see John 16:7-15).

Without an ascended and exalted Christ, therefore, Christian servanthood would be impossible, for the main operator in our sanctification, the Holy Spirit, would neither be available nor effective. From his heavenly throne, Jesus empowers our service through the Holy Spirit. He helps us serve so that we may glorify God and not ourselves. Jesus' exaltation means we can serve like we were originally made to. Because of Christ's exaltation, we can rest in his work and give him glory as we serve.

**Consummation.** We still have one more supremely dramatic and momentous act of Christ's service to witness: One day he will come again to bring all believers into eternal and perfect union with him in heaven. In this great act of service, we will be gathered and given a resurrection body. We will be united with Christ in a great wedding in heaven, where neither sin nor hardship dwell. There, we will worship and serve God for eternity, even as we enjoy the fruits of his service to us.

# The Expanding Kingdom of Service

So we see that the Kingdom of God is built entirely on acts of service, acts that began at creation and will extend through eternity. After the full unfolding of God's promise was demonstrated in the gospel, the impact of Christ's work has grown over time, as those who are affected and saved by Christ point others to him through acts of service. From the universal Christian Church down to each local body, from the historical Pentecost to the future promise of Christ's return—it is all God's doing. He extends his kingdom one soul at a time, using changed hearts to affect and serve others, in a great chain stretching over thousands of years and affecting countless souls. This kingdom is made real by people like you and me who have tasted the amazing grace of Christ and who, in turn, tangibly demonstrate that grace to others. One act of gospel-motivated service begets another, and on and on, until eventually Christ will call the whole family home for one massive celebration.

Romans 5:18 states, "Therefore, as [Adam's] trespass led to condemnation for all men, so [Christ's] act of righteousness leads to justification and life for all men." This service of Jesus Christ on our behalf is the starting point for every act of service that ever has been or ever will be performed by any

Christian. This family tree of service started with Christ and grows continually, spreading its roots, extending its branches, and changing lives forever.

Three
# CONTEXT

The Local Church is Our Base for Service

In the history of baseball, Brooks Robinson's fielding at third base was arguably unmatched. He played twenty-three years for the Baltimore Orioles, setting Major League career records for games, putouts, assists, chances, double plays, and fielding percentage.[9] Brooks played in four World Series, winning the MVP in 1970, and was inducted into the Baseball Hall of Fame in 1983. His fielding was as beautiful as it was daunting.

Brooks played and lived baseball simply because he was devoted to the game, and people who watched him could not help but notice. He once said of himself, "I'm a guy who just wanted to see his name in the lineup every day. To me, baseball was a passion to the point of obsession." This passion made Brooks put everything he had into every play. Umpire Ed Hurley once said of Brooks, "He plays third base like he came down from a higher league." Robinson's passion in life was the thrill he received from stopping an impossible grounder, throwing someone out at first from his knees, or turning a double play. The baseball diamond was a place where his dreams were realized and his passions were played out.

Here's where I'm going with this. Despite all of his zeal and drive, Brooks Robinson could not have achieved anything without a field to play on and a group of people who shared his passion for what happened on that field.

This is the power of context.

## We the Field, We the Players

Most of us could make the distinction between a baseball diamond and a football field, or between the activities of baseball players vs. football players. The fields each have a unique shape, and the players behave in very different ways. One kind of field simply won't work for the other sport, and neither sport is possible without players who know the rules and have certain basic skills. That combination — the right kind of field, plus specifically equipped participants — are what make the game possible. How could Brooks have thrown someone out without a first base to throw to and others on the field? The whole activity would have been pointless.

In the same way, the local church creates a context in which a particular form of worship becomes possible. All true, God-honoring worship finds its motivation and power in the finished work of Christ, and therefore can only be expressed by Christians. And when Christians are gathered into a local church, that form of worship called biblical servanthood can be practiced and expressed in ways that are not possible in any other context.

A local church, in its essence, is not a building or a liturgy. It is not a collection of ministries, or a set of shared beliefs and practices. As the language of the New Testament makes clear, a church is composed of *people*. The people, collectively, are the church (the baseball field), and at the same time the people, individually, are the participants (the baseball players). We the people are both.

## We the Church

In the Bible, God's command to serve him is most always associated with a specific context: the gathered presence of his people. Old Testament commands such as Deuteronomy 6:13 and Leviticus 19:5-7 involved the temple, the tabernacle, or public rituals. For us, the tabernacle is no longer in one specific location. Christ has become our tabernacle, and he is among us all (Matthew 18:20). Accordingly, worship has become decentralized; it takes place wherever groups of believers gather to worship God. Essential to that worship is our service to one another that we might become more effective individually as worshipers of God.

In Acts 6, for example, seven men were appointed to serve in a particular local church to satisfy needs within that congregation. A group of widows in the church were being neglected, primarily because the pastors were trying to do too much on their own. So the leaders created a service team to provide food and care to these widows. Not only did this allow the church to care for its own members, it also made reaching out to others possible (Acts 6:7). The church (collectively) provided the platform for people (individually) to worship God by serving others, thus sustaining and building the church while drawing attention to the glory and grace of God. This was just one very early example of how God designed the church to be his earthly instrument for accomplishing his plan of salvation and sanctification. In fact, as Paul tells us in Ephesians 3, this is the very purpose of the church.

> To me, though I am the very least of all the saints, this grace was given, to preach to the Gentiles the unsearchable riches of Christ, and to bring to light for everyone what is the plan of the mystery hidden for ages in God who created all things, so that through the church the manifold wisdom of God might now be made known to the rulers

and authorities in the heavenly places. This was according to the eternal purpose that he has realized in Christ Jesus our Lord…

Ephesians 3:8-11a

Our adoption into the kingdom of God saves us individually to God, but also saves us into fellowship with each other (Ephesians 2:17-2). God's people are brought together to glorify and worship him in localized, unified expressions of faith that display the wisdom of God's plan of salvation. The Bible commands us to continue meeting together so that we may encourage one another as we seek to live out that plan (Hebrews 10:25). Indeed, Scripture contains more than fifty commands about relating to "one another" in grace-filled, redemptive ways. How can we obey these and so many other passages if we are not among other people? The church is the platform from which we can obey these commands and, in our grace-motivated efforts to do so, present to the world a testimony of God's goodness and mercy.

First Peter 4:10 states, "As each has received a gift, use it to serve one another, as good stewards of God's varied grace." Just as a forward in soccer needs a goal net to provide context for a score, our "serving gifts" need the context of one another—the local church—to bring benefit to others. The church provides the primary context for this stewardship of "God's varied grace."

The church is also a venue through which believers are equipped for ministry, both theologically and practically. Paul tells the church, "And he gave the apostles, the prophets, the evangelists, the pastors and teachers, *to equip the saints for the work of ministry, for building up the body of Christ*, until we all attain to the unity of the faith and of the knowledge of the Son of God" (Ephesians 4:11-16). Clearly, being properly equipped for works in ministry is an essential part of the Christian life, and God intends for this equipping to take place in local churches.

Of course there can be different fields of service such as the workplace, your neighborhood, or some civic context; these are not to be marginalized. Yet, the church stands in a unique position because it is through the church that God "communicates his manifold wisdom." If the church is primary context for dispensing specific means of grace such as the Word and Sacraments, then the church is also the primary context for the expression of the effects and privileges of this grace. Without a local body of believers, how could someone grow in his or her ability to minister to others? How could anyone truly help build the body of Christ apart from active membership and sincere participation in a local expression of that body?

# This Beautiful Mess

Besides all these good things, the church, as we all know, can be a very messy place. After all, it's full of sinners! Each and every one of us are real people with real and often inconvenient problems. We may be tempted to grumble when our efforts to serve get tangled up in the mess, but a life without messiness and inconvenience is a life without true service. God is calling us to serve despite our inconvenience and discomfort, because his top priority is the glory he will receive as our lives become more and more conformed to his image. He wants to do real work in the church — through us — to help clean up the mess that is our collective sin.

The beautiful thing is that God meets us in the mess. People are served in the mess. Ultimately, Christ will redeem the mess. One reason the church is the primary context for serving is because it is where messy people go when they know they need help. Through salvation and hope in Christ we have glimpsed the depth of our own sin. We have seen something of our own mess.

What we must remember, especially when it gets really messy, is that no amount of mess will ever invalidate the church's place as the principal context for service to God and one another. God calls us to serve regardless of the mess. He uses our service to address not only the mess, but messed-up people.

Ultimately, service begins and finds its fulfillment in the church, for if we cannot care for our own family, how can we care effectively for others? How can we bring those who are outside the church into a divided, dysfunctional family? The church is the base from which God's people go out to serve a messy world, and it is the place we encourage the hurting and the lost to come to in order to see God at work. Working on our own messes inside the church is essential to our mission.

## A Diverse Unity

Servanthood involves caring for people (even when that means caring for material goods such as church buildings). But all that service to people (and things) is ultimately service to God. As God serves through us, the glory always comes back around to him.

Professor Edmund Clowney writes, "The church is called to serve God in three ways: to serve him directly in worship; to serve the saints in nurture; and to serve the world in witness."[10] When naturally selfish human beings behave as biblical servants, it draws attention to God, demonstrating that his grace changes hearts. In this way, God's glory is proclaimed and manifested through serving.

Generally speaking, the local church provides two distinct contexts or positions for serving: structured and spontaneous. *Structured* positions are not limited to pastors, elders, deacons, ushers, and the like. These positions involve anything that is staffed and scheduled. Structured positions allow for things to be done "decently and in order" (1 Corinthians 14:40).

*Spontaneous* service, on the other hand, involves unplanned acts that are not usually regulated by the church in any formal way. These are often deeds done in private, like bringing meals, writing encouragement notes, praying for someone, or even just holding the door open for someone. Spontaneous services are everyday acts of magnifying and living the gospel. They can be done almost anytime by almost anyone, and provide a flexibility and range of service that a structured system could never duplicate.

Sharon is a living model of spontaneous servanthood. She suffers terribly from fibromyalgia, spending most of her time in bed and in pain, and is rarely able to attend church or small-group meetings. In the four years that I have known her, I have only seen her a few times. But from her bed, Sharon offers housing to singles in the church, and opens her home for weekly swim parties and care-group events. She writes letters of encouragement and prays for people. Some have gone to help clean her home and come away feeling like *they* were the ones who'd been served.

Examples like Sharon's help us realize that the

various ways we can serve one another are simply echoes of how the three persons of the Trinity carry out their individual roles. The Father created the world and planned salvation. The Son came to earth and redeemed us. The Holy Spirit works to change us through sanctification. All three roles are necessary to carry out God's plan. Our relationships and forms of service can and should mirror this example of unity within diversity.

Paul explained this very thought to the church in Rome:

> For as in one body we have many members, and the members do not all have the same function, so we, though many, are one body in Christ, and individually members one of another. Having gifts that differ according to the grace given to us, let us use them: if prophecy, in proportion to our faith; if service, in our serving; the one who teaches, in his teaching; the one who exhorts, in his exhortation; the one who contributes, in generosity; the one who leads, with zeal; the one who does acts of mercy, with cheerfulness.
>
> Romans 12:4-8

Each of us has various talents, experiences, and traditions. Yet we are to act in unity and harmony out of love for God and one another. It is through, not despite, our diversity that we love and serve others. "The gifts of the Spirit do differ, but they never divide," writes Edmund Clowney, "for they enable the church to function as an organism, the body of Christ… Organic unity requires diversity of function."

While every Christian's acts of service will be different, they are unified with a common purpose—a love that springs from the God of love. Sharon cannot lead worship, teach in children's ministry, or greet guests, but she can show the grace and love of God by the means God has given her. The worship is the same in heart, yet different in expression.

## Purpose, Not Perfection

In the big picture, the hallmark of the Christian life is not about how well-organized or structured (or, for that matter, how spontaneous) the church is. Rather, it is whether we have built our faith, our church, and our ministries on the foundation of the gospel. A passion for the local church should stem not from *our* work in the church, but from *Christ's* passion, plans for, and work in the local church. When this is the taproot from which we draw nourishment, we can serve and love one another motivated by God's grace, propelled by his love, and enabled by his Spirit. As we begin to understand and live this, we develop a stronger desire to minister, and our serving metamorphoses into a passionate drive to see God glorified and the gospel magnified in people's lives.

Through the practice of servanthood-as-worship in local churches, believers and the lost alike come to more clearly taste and see God's provision and love. As chairs are arranged, children watched, books sold, instruments played, local outreaches conducted, prayers prayed, and Bible studies taught, a great testimony of praise is offered up. "In the pursuit of holiness, in the proclamation of the Gospel, in the service of the poor and friendless, the church of Christ builds a spiritual culture, a foretaste of the kingdom to come. Life [is] transformed in a community living in love for God and our neighbors."[11]

While this book is intended to encourage Christians to be more active in our high calling to serve, our God is neither a taskmaster nor a tyrant. He does not expect or require all Christians, no matter their circumstances, to serve in the church continually. There is a time for everything, including rest and respite (Ecclesiastes 3). Sometimes, especially in seasons where personal burdens grow unusually heavy, it is perfectly fine to feel released from serving, and we should extend this grace to others just as God does to us. Indeed, those who are hurting in the church should first and foremost be served by the church.

By the same token, God is not after a perfect
record of service or a superhuman demonstration
of unflagging passion. He knows we are weak and
tempted to sinful behaviors. In a meeting with a
service team at my church, I asked everyone why
he or she served. An astute teenager said something
I have always remembered: "When serving has
become duty to me, that usually means God has
become a duty as well." Every one of us is going to
have seasons where serving feels like nothing but
duty. None of us will ever be the Brooks Robinson
of local-church servants. But we don't need to be
all-stars with world-class skills and unbelievable
consistency. That is why we have Jesus who, "being
made perfect ... became the source of eternal
salvation to all who obey him" (Hebrews 5:9). God
simply wants our worship. Our perfection he
already supplied in Christ.

Four
# GLORY

God's Character and Works

Six nautical miles off the coast of Suffolk,
England, the Principality of Sealand does not have
a visitors' bureau, nor does it tolerate tourism.
There's not much to see, anyway—its territory
consists of an abandoned World War II fort rising
out of the international waters of the English
Channel. Sealand's 550 square meters is home to a
grand total of five people. Their Royal Highnesses,
Prince Roy Bates and his wife, Princess Joan Bates,
founded the micro-nation in 1967 when they began
operating a pirate radio broadcast from the fort.
They soon claimed sovereignty by creating Sealand's
Constitution, which conveniently includes the
hereditary succession of the monarchy.

What qualified "Paddy" Roy Bates to become
a king, even if his kingdom is little more than a
large shed on a concrete slab perched above the
English Channel? Other than having an active

imagination and some initiative, nothing qualified him, really. Sealand is simply one of the more unusual expressions of the universal desire to rule over something, anything, as long as we can call it our own.

All of us are busy building our little kingdoms. In our imaginary principalities, we are the sovereign rulers, deserving of honor and worship from the lesser beings around us. And while Sealand may be easy to scoff at, that's only because Paddy Bates went public about what was going on in his heart. In truth, our own kingdoms are no less pitiful, no less fanciful, no less absurd. What we all resist recognizing and acknowledging is that ultimately all rulership belongs to One. All glory belongs to a single King. On our own, we rule and control precisely nothing.

What we call rulership, God calls stewardship. If we have genuine authority over anything, it is only because that authority has been delegated to us by God. We did not create whatever little kingdom we call our own, and we do not truly rule over its affairs. God does. He is the one King, and to him belongs all glory.

## God of Glory

God's glory is not a simple thing to understand or express in all its fullness. But, without pretending that this is the entire explanation, we can say that his glory is bound in and springs forth from his *character* and is seen in his *works*.

**Character.** God is completely perfect, in both the negative and the positive senses. That is, on the one hand, he is devoid of both mistakes and moral corruption, and on the other hand, he possesses all purity, knowledge, and power. God lacks nothing in his own being or in his abilities. His perfection is limited by neither time nor space. Every created thing, man included, is crippled by limitations and contaminated by sin. Only God—the very definition of goodness and power—is worthy of our ultimate worship.

**Work of Creation.** God's character is more than enough to endow him with endless glory. Yet in addition to that character, we have the evidence of creation. Indeed, creation was brought into existence specifically to draw attention to God's preeminent and pre-existing glory.

And what a creation it is. Recall Genesis 1:1 — "In the beginning, God created the heavens and the earth." Let's try something. Put down this book, close your eyes, and repeat that verse to yourself, slowly. Think about it. Then open your eyes and take a good, long look around you. Consider also the many wonders that you cannot see. God created it all, from the breath in your lungs, to the ground beneath you, to the virtually limitless sky above you, containing hundreds of times more *galaxies* than there are human beings on this planet. God created every molecule, neutron, and quark.

In awe at God and his creation, the author of Psalm 96 writes an impassioned explanation of the unique majesty of God. He urges us to ascribe to God the glory rightfully due him. The psalmist starts by encouraging the entire planet to praise God and declare his works among the nations. Then he continues, "For great is the Lord, and greatly to be praised; he is to be feared above all gods. For all the gods of the peoples are worthless idols, but the Lord made the heavens. Splendor and majesty are before him; strength and beauty are in his sanctuary" (Psalm 96:4-6). God is unique. He is the one who with a word formed a universe of inconceivable complexity. His majesty, glory, and power stand unmatched.

**Work of Salvation.** God also demonstrates his glory by accomplishing our eternal salvation in Christ. God sent his only Son to be our substitute and pay the penalty our sins deserved. Paul writes, "For our sake he made him to be sin who knew no sin, so that in him we might become the righteousness of God" (2 Corinthians 5:21). Through Christ's sacrifice and imputed righteousness, we now have unlimited and eternal access to this holy, loving, and supremely glorious God. As the apostle Jude writes, "to the only God, our Savior, through Jesus Christ our Lord, be glory, majesty, dominion, and authority, before all time and now and forever. Amen" (Jude 1:25).

## Servanthood as Worship

If our God were not glorious in both his character and works, where would be the joy in serving him? What would there be to excite our emotions, to provoke us to wonder and amazement, or to inspire us to serve? If our God had no glory in himself, he would merely be bizarre and terrifying, a despot who is respected only because he's powerful. A god like that would actually have a lot in common with the ruler of Sealand—just with a much bigger fort.

But God *is* glorious, and his glory is the inexhaustible fuel and the thrilling focus of Christian service. Our calling is to interact with both God and his creation aware of his glory, empowered by his glory, and in magnification of his glory. As a response to his glory, we seek to reflect that glory back to him. We worship God through serving God.

Perhaps this helps shed some light on one of my fundamental points in this book: that servanthood is intertwined with and indistinguishable from worship in the true, broad sense of the word. Most Christians understand *worship* quite narrowly, associating it almost exclusively with that time on

Sunday morning when we all sing together. For some Christians, *worship* is shorthand for the entire Sunday meeting, including and especially the preaching of God's Word. These certainly are worship, and very special forms of it, but ultimately they are only a tiny portion of the whole.

Paul explodes the definition of worship to its true dimensions when he writes, "So, whether you eat or drink, or whatever you do, do all to the glory of God" 1 Corinthians 10:31. Worship can encompass all of life—every thought, every moment, every word. This is why we can say confidently that servanthood is worship and, when done with the right motivations, one of the highest forms of it.

Puritan pastor and author Thomas Watson writes, "We glorify God when we are devoted to his service; our head studies for him, our tongue pleads for him, and our hands relieve his members."[12] The apostle Peter shares this exact sentiment in 1 Peter 4:10-11.

> As each has received a gift, use it to serve one another, as good stewards of God's varied grace: whoever speaks, as one who speaks oracles of God; whoever serves, as one who serves by the strength that God supplies—in order that in everything God may be glorified through Jesus Christ. To him belong glory and dominion forever and ever. Amen.

Thus, it is not the outward task that defines worship, it is the inward devotion to God and a desire to glorify him. Even the smallest, most mundane act can be worship. Christian service is worship in action.

# A Grateful Response

When we don't fully understand service, we can be tempted to re-define it to suit our current situation. We shift our point of reference—our way of understanding service—from what the Bible says to what we prefer to believe. That's when we fall back into seeing service as a salvation-meriting work, a means of penance, or a necessary evil of church life. I've been at all those places more than once, haven't you? But the fact is that *biblical* servanthood is a reaction to God, a response to a holy God's forgiveness of our sins. We do not serve *for* salvation, but *from* salvation. Serving is intended to magnify the gospel, not replace it. Our serving is a manifestation, an outworking, an evidence of our faith in Christ.

Once we grasp this truth, it changes our view of service in the church. Then, when facing a surprise request to serve in the nursery, or to perform some unglamorous task, our response can be quite different. We are less likely to think, *How is this helping me?* Instead, we are more likely to respond with a heart of God-centered service.

For the next four chapters, we're going to imitate Thomas Watson by examining some biblically grounded attitudes that can help keep our service on track. Watson writes, "Glorifying God consists in four things: 1. Appreciation, 2. Adoration, 3. Affection, 4. Subjection."[13] Following this outline, we will examine how serving glorifies God when it *appreciates* God's glorious character and works; *adores* his presence; shares God's *affection* towards his people; and *subjects* itself to his will.

## Five
# APPRECIATION

I Can Serve Because I Appreciate Who God Is,
Who I Am, and What He Has Done for Me

My dad is a rabid cartophile. He loves maps and has owned hundreds of them. He's not merely a collector. He studies and uses his maps, extracting their encoded information and sharing it with whoever will listen. I remember flying across the country, sitting in the window seat with him next to me. Every now and then he would lean over to peer out the window, clutching a map and pointing out places of interest. When he is armed with maps, being on a trip with my father can be a little like traveling with a semi-omniscient tour guide.

Whenever my dad studies a map, he uses his favorite magnifying glass. In watching him indulge his love of maps through the years, I have noticed something. He only uses the glass to magnify the area he is most interested in. It occurs to me now that this is a picture of how we all live.

As my father sits with a map spread before him, there are so many things he could focus on. But usually he does have a focus. There is some particular area that has his attention. So he picks up the glass and magnifies that one area. We do the same—we look out over our lives and we focus on something. That's what we give our attention to. That's what we want to learn more about. As we do so, it becomes much bigger to us, and much more important compared to the other things on our personal "map."

In paying attention to this area, we have magnified it. This is nothing less than an act of worship, an act of service, because it represents a sacrifice of our time, energy, interest, and passion that could have gone elsewhere. Just like the glass magnifies a place on a map, the way we live and serve magnifies our dreams, values, ambitions, and motivations. What we focus on becomes bigger to us. Our focusing produces our worship.

In light of this, how do we focus our primary attention on God, that we might serve him more than anything else? How can we make sure that our service, especially in the local church, magnifies the only one who is truly worthy?

*We can serve effectively in our local church when we appreciate who God is, who we are, and what he has done for us. Serving is not to be done for God, but primarily because of God.*

## Appreciating Who God Is

Glorifying God starts with appreciating him. However, we cannot appreciate a God we do not know. Pastor John Stott explains, "The first fundamental principle of Christian worship, [is] namely that we must know God before we can worship him … It is impossible to worship an unknown God, since, if he himself is unknown, the kind of worship he desires will be equally unknown."[14]

This is exactly Jesus' point to Martha in Luke 10:38-42. In this passage, Jesus tells Martha to stop serving and just sit down and listen to him. Jesus is not explaining to Martha how to serve; he is inviting her to get to know the God she's serving. (Notice also that he is not telling her to stop worshiping, simply to change the form of her worship.) God wants our hearts and affections—not only our service—and to reach them he must have our attention.

Just like Martha, as we come know God, we start to understand his worthiness and majesty. From there, it is only natural that we seek to glorify him. Jesus is demonstrating, to Martha and to us, that the essential thing about our servanthood is its motivation. What area of our personal map are we actually magnifying? What has our attention? Where are we focused? Knowledge of God and his works is the starting point for true service.

How are we to gain such knowledge? Although we cannot physically sit at the feet of Jesus, God has made more than sufficient provision for us. J.I Packer states, "We must say that knowing God involves first listening to God's Word."[15] The Bible tells us all we could possibly know in this life about the Father, Son, and Holy Spirit.

The Bible is the primary means by which we come to know God. It is in God's Word that we see his character, his ways, our condition, and the eternal hope of Christ (1 Corinthians 15). Paul writes, "For whatever was written in former days was written for our instruction, that through endurance and through the encouragement of the Scriptures we might have hope" (Romans 15:4). God establishes and fosters his relationship with us through his Word (Luke 6:47-48). It is primarily through his Word that we can come to truly appreciate God (Psalm 119). This appreciation for God can then transform our service into worship of God, as we take the magnifying glass off ourselves and place it on God and the truth of Scripture.

## Appreciating Who We Are

In order to glorify God as we serve, we must also appreciate who *we* are. "We cannot seriously aspire to him," writes Calvin, in a discussion about knowing God, "before we begin to become displeased with ourselves."[16] In appreciating who we are, we must first understand the dire predicament the natural man is in. Scripture is essential here as well, teaching us about what theologians call Original Sin and Total Depravity.

**Original Sin.** The Bible tells us that when Adam sinned, his disobedience and the guilt of his sin was counted against his descendants (Romans 5:18-19). This is known as Original Sin. Because of it we all have Adam's guilt imputed to us, we are all held liable for Adam's sin. Therefore, the punishment due to him is due to us as well.

**Total Depravity.** The bad news doesn't stop there, either, because each of us is also guilty of our own sinful acts. Our natural state is so infected with sin that we cannot change it or, in ourselves, even genuinely *want* to change it. Because of what we have inherited from Adam, we are naturally slaves to sin (Romans 6:19), indulging happily in its unholy pleasures (Ephesians 2:1-5). The common theological term for the underlying cause of this condition is Total Depravity. This phrase doesn't mean we are as bad as we could possibly be, or that we are incapable of any moral good. But it does mean that sin has affected every *area* of life. That's why the unsaved sinner is totally unable to please God or to alter his or her basic preference for sin and self-gratification.[17] Even as Christians, we sin on a daily basis because we carry within us this sin nature, infected by and inherited from the first man, Adam. We are, all of us, unable *not* to sin.

Taken together, our original sin and total depravity pose a potent problem for us. Scripture teaches that God cannot tolerate sin (Habakkuk 1:13). As the Puritan-era writer Ralph Venning puts it, "It [sin] goes about to ungod God."[18] Sin and God are wholly and utterly incompatible. God's pervasive holiness demands pervasive justice for sin. Pastor John Murray explains, "God cannot be indifferent to or complacent towards that which is the contradiction of himself. His very perfection requires the recoil of righteous indignation. And that is God's wrath."[19] As a consequence, sin—and thereby the sinner—must be punished by death (Romans 6:23).

Our *sin* makes us rebellious outlaws, deserving of God's just wrath. Our *depravity* makes loving God impossible on our own. Our *corruption* renders us unable to save ourselves from God's justice. When asked, "Who could be saved?" Jesus responds, "With man this is impossible" (Matthew 19:26). We are under God's wrath (Ephesians 2:3) and unable to escape it.

As we read the Bible and examine our own behaviors and weaknesses, we begin to appreciate who we are—not in a joyful way, but with a soberness and desperation that leads us to cry out for help as Job does in Job 31.

Until we grasp what we are, we will never ask for what we need—a Savior.

## Appreciating What God Has Done for Us

Luke brings us the account of a brief conversation that Jesus had with one of the two criminals being crucified alongside him (Luke 23:39-43). When the one thief expressed faith in Jesus, Jesus assured him that he would be saved. I suspect this account appears in Scripture to demonstrate the fact that we can do nothing to earn our salvation. Like a man nailed to a cross, we are utterly unable to serve our way into God's favor. Salvation comes only as a gift, never as a payment for services rendered.

The good news of the gospel is that what is impossible with man *is* possible with God. Where we could never earn salvation, Jesus *could* and *did* earn it—and actually as a kind of payment for services rendered. That's amazing enough in itself. But then he granted us the benefit of his accomplishment, even when we were as weak and helpless and condemned to death as that bleeding criminal on a cross.

This is why salvation is found solely in the person of Jesus Christ and his selfless service to us.

Rather than being based upon our own good works, our salvation was purchased for us by Another (Ephesians 2:8-9).

By understanding and savoring this third and final truth, we are able to serve in a way that truly brings glory to God. Appreciating what God has done for us in Christ changes how we see our service. Martin Luther writes, "Thus from faith flow forth love and joy in the Lord, and from love a cheerful, willing, free spirit, disposed to serve our neighbor voluntarily, without taking any account of gratitude or ingratitude, praise or blame, gain or loss."[20]

As the Spirit operates through the Word of God to give us a clear understanding of who we are, who God is, and what God has done for us in Christ, the gospel will increasingly inspire our service, define our service, and be reflected in our service. Service becomes a grateful response to Christ's sacrificial service to us. We no longer think of serving as an effort to earn favor with God, but as an effort to magnify the One who granted us his favor as a gift.

## Six
# ADORATION

I Can Serve as I Desire and Enjoy
God's Active Presence

If you have read much history, you may be familiar with the Forlorn Hope. This was a 19th Century military term for those who made up the first wave of assault against formidable enemy defenses. The basic idea is commonly seen in movies involving large-scale armed conflict. Think of the U-boats on D-Day disgorging those first soldiers onto the beaches of Normandy in *Saving Private Ryan*. Or the initial assault on Helm's Deep in *The Lord of the Rings*. Or the attempted storming of Fort Wagner in *Glory*. They all have one thing in common: When you're starting from a position of weakness, the first wave of combatants is considered lost before the encounter even begins. When you are a member of a Forlorn Hope, the deck is horribly stacked against you. You're basically doomed from the start, stuck in a situation you can't avoid and can't win.

At times, when we consider what God requires of us, it can feel a little like we, too, have enlisted in a Forlorn Hope. We may begin from a place of great joy over our salvation but at some point, as we begin to realize God's requirements, we begin to see things differently. We look at the "hill" of God's commands and realize we can't climb it. We're simply not capable. And God's Word is terribly clear. If you don't climb that hill, it's over. You're dead, in the worst possible way.

Let's briefly review the "field of engagement." God has placed many unbending requirements on humanity. These include the Ten Commandments, the Sermon on the Mount, and the "do unto others" golden rule, to mention only a few. If we are being at all honest, we will recognize that simply loving our fellow man in every situation and at all times is impossible even for one busy day, let alone a lifetime. The apostle Paul, a man with far more spiritual insight than any of us, knew that the failure rate in obeying God is 100 percent, "for all have sinned and fall short of the glory of God" (Romans 3:23).

As Christians, we rejoice in the fact that there is an answer to this dilemma. It's the truth that saved us, and the truth we must remind ourselves of every day. Jesus Christ did climb the hill. He did everything perfectly, obeying all of God's commands with his heart, mind, and strength, and God the Father ascribes his obedience to us.

That's all well and good. It really is the best news we could ever have. But the forlorn hope I'm talking about involves more than salvation. It's true that the Father and the Son have solved the problem of our eternal destination. But what about today, and tomorrow, and the day after that? What about our ongoing efforts on *this* side of eternity? Christ has taken care of the ultimate outcome, but what about the countless little outcomes between now and then? What about that rainy Sunday morning when you don't want to go drive the van? Or that surprise request to serve in the nursery? When faced with the challenge to serve cheerfully and graciously, we can still be tempted to feel like we have enlisted in a Forlorn Hope and face an impossible task. What do we do about that?

God has made a way here, too. He wants us to expand our vision to encompass even *more* of what he has done. The Son died for us. The Father counts us righteous in the Son. But we get into trouble, especially with respect to daily realities like serving in the local church, if we forget the role of the *third* Person of the Trinity—the Holy Spirit.

## The Spirit: God's Active Presence

The Holy Spirit first acts to draw us to Christ, and then to save and equip us. Our spiritual awakening could never have occurred had not the Spirit first done his work in our hearts. After our conversion, the Spirit dwells within us (John 14:16-17). Throughout this life, he continues to work in us, piercing the veil of sin and convicting our conscience of sins we commit (John 16:7-9). He also unfolds for us something of God's majesty and glory, primarily through the illumination of Scripture. This appreciation of God and his works is what motivates our service. We cannot desire to serve God unless we have a glimpse of his magnificence, and only through the Spirit can we gain that right understanding of God.

But let's assume that somehow we had full intellectual knowledge of God's glory. Even then, if we were merely operating under our own power, it would still be impossible to be the servants God calls us to be. We need something potent and external to help us. That something is in fact a Someone. Ever since Pentecost, the Spirit has been the active presence of God in the lives and hearts of Christians.

Because of Pentecost, we now live in "the new way of the Spirit" (Romans 7:6 ). God's continued activity through the Holy Spirit leads us both to worship God and to find joy in serving others. Our delight in and adoration of God grows as we begin to experience the Spirit's work in us. Each taste of God's grace provokes a desire for more. As that progression takes its course, serving in the church can become a true joy, because we are no longer trying to serve exclusively under our own power. Instead, God's active presence is providing a *desire* and an *effectiveness* that we could never produce or maintain on our own.

This empowering joy is rooted in the experience of being forgiven and adopted by God. It manifests itself in a delight to magnify God's glory by serving him. This practical, joyful expression of love for God is the essence of adoration. As we reflect on God's work in us, our adoration for him should increase and overflow through joyful service. We feel so much joy that we can't wait to spread it around!

Someone recently asked me, "Do we serve to find joy, or do we serve because there is joy?" The answer is: Both! We begin with an inner joy produced by the grace of the Gospel—joy *for* serving. We also find joy by participating in God's plan to benefit others—joy *in* serving. Psalm 16:11 says, "You make known to me the path of life; in your presence there is fullness of joy; at your right hand are pleasures forevermore." There is inherent and limitless joy as we enter into the presence of the eternal, all-powerful, yet gracious King who has allowed undeserving people like you and me into the kingdom of heaven. That is why C.J. Mahaney can write, "Joy is a command. You may be working hard and serving the Lord faithfully, but if you aren't serving with gladness, you aren't serving him appropriately or representing him accurately."[21]

Through the Holy Spirit's activity we come to love God, his Word, his work, and his people. The Spirit plants adoration for God in our hearts. It is the cultivation and exercise of this joyful adoration that empowers us for service.

## Gifted to Serve

The Holy Spirit, God's active presence within and among us, does more than convict us of sin, illuminate the Word of God to us, and enable us to serve. He also gives each of us one or more specific gifts of service, and enables us to recognize and develop those gifts. Speaking of spiritual gifts, Paul says, "All these are empowered by one and the same Spirit, who apportions to each one individually as he wills" (1 Corinthians 12:11). Peter adds, "As each has received a gift, use it to serve one another, as good stewards of God's varied grace" (1 Peter 4:10).

Peter is not identifying a "gift of service" that some people have but others do not. He is saying that God has given *each* Christian certain gifts, and we are *all* called to put our gifts to use in ways that serve God and others. First Corinthians 12:7 makes it plain: "To each is given the manifestation of the Spirit for the common good." Martin Luther writes in *Concerning Christian Liberty*, "You see, then, that, if we recognize those great and precious gifts, as Peter says, which have been given to us, love is quickly diffused in our hearts through the Spirit, and by love we are made free, joyful, all-powerful, active workers, victors over all our tribulations, servants to our neighbor, and nevertheless lords of all things."[22] The "manifestation of the Spirit" may look different for each Christian, but Scripture could not be more clear that service is a hallmark of the Christian life, not a rare and unusual gifting. We are called to serve one another in precisely the same sense we are called to love one another. The two are inextricably bound.

Gene Veith Jr., in his book *God at Work*, could have been thinking about the idea of a Forlorn Hope when he wrote, "And yet for all of our sin, we nevertheless serve and help others even against our will—not of ourselves, but because of the power God exerts in our vocations."[23] This is the work of the Holy Spirit, who gives us the power to serve others even when we really, really don't want to. Hardships, obstacles, and sin are always with us, blocking and stunting our passion to serve God. Things like financial or relational troubles can cause us to become self-obsessed. When trials come knocking, we are tempted to just quit serving God and start serving ourselves again—and apart from cultivating the work of the Spirit in our lives, that's exactly what we will do.

# The Power of Adoration

We simply cannot empower ourselves to serve God and one another. But the Holy Spirit acts as our helper to encourage and remind us of what we have in Christ. He helps us realize how rich we are in Christ and how loved we are by our heavenly Father. Through the Hoy Spirit, God helps us transform service from duty into worship, and forlorn hope into joy.

Your hope is a solid one. You have been given God himself in the person of the Holy Spirit to empower you to serve with consistent joy in the light of who God is and what he has done for you. Your conscience, purified by the blood of Christ and informed by the Spirit, can now turn from the dead works of living for self to vital works of living for God. The more we adore God, desiring and enjoying the Spirit's work and power in our lives, the more we will step out of our comfort zones and serve. The Spirit is the agent by whom we serve, and as such is essential to Christian service. Thank God for the Holy Spirit, who opens our eyes and causes us to reflect on and adore Christ, our eternal hope.

## Seven
# AFFECTION

I Can Serve Motivated by Love for the Saved and Unsaved

The Vegan Society was created to "promote vegan lifestyles—that is, ways of living that seek to exclude, as far as is possible and practical, all forms of exploitation of animals for food, clothing, or any other purpose."[24] It's probably safe to say, therefore, that you will never find a vegan butcher. Chopping up dead animals so other people can cook and eat them is totally incompatible with vegan philosophy. You cannot be a butcher and a true vegan at the same time—it is a contradiction in terms. Such a person would either cease to be a vegan or else be a really ineffective butcher.

Likewise, a Christian without some evidence of genuine affection for other people is also a contradiction. We know this because the Bible both tells us and shows us that God is the very definition of love (1 John 4:10). "God is love, from

Himself, and not from another; He is absolutely, independently love . . . it is His essence itself," writes Octavius Winslow.[25] If we are to glorify God and rightly represent him to this world, how can we not express this unique and wondrous trait? That is why 1 Corinthians 13:1-2 expresses how, without love, Christians are nothing more than a noisy gong, those who preach love but do not display it.

In the previous chapter we were reminded of the ever-present help we have in the person of the Holy Spirit. Here we will see that, because of that same Spirit, we can be motivated to serve by the power of God's love for people—people inside and outside the church. And, following up on a brief mention of the subject in chapter three, we will see that looking to the Trinity is essential for an accurate understanding of our role as individuals within the collective we call the church.

## The Nature of God's Love

The God of the Bible is not a group of gods, but rather one God comprising three distinct persons. The Westminster Shorter Catechism states, "There are three Persons in the Godhead; the Father, the Son, and the Holy Spirit; and these three are one God, the same in substance, equal in power and glory."[26] The threefold nature of God implies that a relationship exists between each member of the Godhead. We can think of a relationship as the interactions and mutual interests that exist between two or more persons. God is in relationship to himself. Indeed, the triune nature of God, in its essence, *is* a relationship.

If God is a trinity, and God is love, we can be sure of this: the Trinity is characterized by relationships of perfect, communal, and indwelling love among its members. These relationships are flawless in every respect. There is no bickering or jealousy, no uncertainty or fears, no suspicion or questioning of motives. There is only mutual, unchanging love and eternal, unbroken unity. It is, we might say, heaven.

That's a thrilling subject in itself, but right now we want to focus on what that means for us as God's people.

When we become Christians we enter into fellowship with our God who is a divine, tri-fold union, three persons in one God. Through our fellowship with God, we also come into union with God's people. We need to see that this *necessarily* happens. Through the death and resurrection of Christ, God has created a people bound together through his blood (Ephesians 2:18-22). Salvation brings us to God, but also to his people. It is inescapable, part of the package. We have been saved by a God who is a divine community. As a result, we become part of a human community that is itself joined to that divine community at both the individual level and the corporate level.

Fundamental to our purpose as Christians, therefore, is to love one another and the world with the love of the Trinity in an ongoing, increasingly accurate way. Pastor John Stott writes, "Thus the very purpose of [Christ's] self-giving on the cross was not just to save individuals, and so perpetuate their loneliness, but to create a new community whose members would belong to him, love one another, and eagerly serve the world."[27]

Love is the basis of the triune God's internal relationships. It is the basis of his relationships with us. Clearly, as Christians, it is also the foundation of and model for our relationships with others. John goes so far as to say that when we love others, God's image is perfected in us (1 John 4:11-12). Paul writes, "And walk in love, as Christ loved us and gave himself up for us, a fragrant offering and sacrifice to God" (Ephesians 5:2). In this verse, we see that loving others really does involve the full Trinity: the Son's sacrifice, the Father's acceptance, and the Spirit's work. By the power of the perfect love that exists within the triune God, he enables us to establish loving and service-oriented relationships with others.

## Love within the Church

Christian love and service are one. In Colossians 3:11-15, we can see two things. First, that we are bound to Christ and subsequently to one another in the body of Christ, the Church. Second, that Christ's love and care for his own body should therefore become our love and care. To the Galatians, Paul says, "For you were called to freedom, brothers. Only do not use your freedom as an opportunity for the flesh, but through love serve one another" (Galatians 5:13).

*Through love serve* — in this phrase, love and service could not be more closely joined. Biblical service *is* the tangible expression of biblical love. We are to serve one another through the kind of divine love that finds its origin in the Trinity. God willingly gave his only Son up to die and endure the wrath of sin because of love for the world (John 3:16). Serving is thus more than an activity; it is sharing God's love. Acts of "service" done begrudgingly, halfheartedly, or resentfully fall short of the biblical standard. Genuine love and genuine service are not independent from one another. They cannot be separated.

**Christian love, unity, and service are mutually reinforcing.** Christians are called to manifest God's love within the church in ways that are a little different from how that love is to be manifested outside the church. In both venues we seek to glorify God by serving selflessly. Within the church, however, we also love and serve as part of an effort to increase unity. Christ himself prayed to the Father that God's people may be one even as he is one within the Trinity (John 17:10b). As we serve one another in love, we cooperate with God in pursuing the ultimate answer to that prayer.

We start from the foundation of the familial bond we share as children of God. This sense of shared kinship in Christ should compel us to serve, even if we are new to a particular local church, or even if we only serve in small ways at first.

Serving someone, meeting them at a point of need and helping them to carry their burden, can be a particularly effective way to get to know someone at a deep and meaningful level. Of course, not every act of service is this directly personal. Much of the serving necessary in local churches involves equipment and facilities more than people. Yet even these efforts contribute to unity by creating a harmonious and orderly context for church meetings. As needs both practical and personal are provided for within a community, people naturally come to trust and love each other all the more.

As we are knit together into a local expression of Christ's body, the well-being of our fellow church members becomes increasingly important to us. "We are driven to consider not only what the Lord calls us to *do* together, but also what he calls us to *be* together,"[28] writes Edmund Clowney. Through this loving sense of care we can increasingly meet one another's needs in ways that are not ultimately self-serving.

This produces relationships that further ignite our *desire* to serve. Paul states in 1 Thessalonians 2:8, "So, being affectionately desirous of you, we were ready to share with you not only the gospel of God but also our own selves, because you had become very dear to us." Because Paul and his companions had developed a passion for the Thessalonians, they were ready to share everything with that church, chancing their very lives. Such love should characterize and define us.

In sum, biblical serving, the kind that springs from love and is done for the glory of God, furthers unity in the local church. In turn, increased unity promotes serving that is more biblical, more extensive, and more wholehearted. The two processes can become so closely intertwined as to be mirror images of one another.

Because each of us has various talents, experiences, and traditions, our forms and expressions of service will differ. The unifying thread running through all of it is mutual love in Christ and a desire to serve in whatever way meets a genuine need. Often we will find ourselves serving in ways that seem to match our talents and gifting, but because church circumstances can differ widely, we should resist seeing that as a test of authentic service. Authentic service is about cooperatively meeting needs, motivated by love, in a unified effort to build the church and glorify God.

## Love Toward the World

"Apart from the life and ministry of Jesus himself," writes James Montgomery Boice, "Christians are to be the best thing that ever happened to this world. We are to be sources of constant good, sharing, love, and service so that the world might be blessed and some (we do not forget this) might come to faith in our Savior."[29] Through our service, we have opportunity to share the love and the message of our Savior with others. We can pursue this in two ways: By welcoming others as Christ welcomed us, and by treating others as Christ treats us.

**Welcome others unconditionally.** Jesus did not wait until you were lovable before he loved and welcomed you. Jesus did not tell me to love my neighbor as myself—except for that guy who offended me, or the girl with the tattoos and eyebrow rings. He does not make exceptions for the homeless, or the prejudiced, or the incarcerated, or the ultra conservative, or the abortion supporter, or the homosexual, or the super-rich, or anyone else. If "the love of Christ controls us" (2 Corinthians 5:14), how can we continue to be controlled by our own comfort and prejudices?

Paul told the Romans, "Welcome one another as Christ has welcomed you, for the glory of God" (Romans 15:7). Although he is talking here primarily about relationships in the church, notice how a welcoming spirit glorifies God—because it emulates God, who welcomed us when nothing about us was welcoming. We are called to welcome those in need, not just those we want to impress, or those with whom we have much in common. Our love and our welcoming is to be like God's—blind to matters of economics, race, nationality, age, religion, or lifestyle.

**Treat others with sacrificial love.** As we seek to carry the love and the message of the cross to those who so desperately need it, some of our service has to take place outside the church, whether this is done as part of a program or simply as part of our lifestyle. On this point, Paul Tripp asks an insightful question. "Could it be that our passivity to the needs around us does not really grow out of a commitment to prioritize what God has commanded us to *do*, but is really a neglect of how he has commanded us to *live*? It is the difference between focusing on specific *behaviors* as opposed to a particular kind of *lifestyle*."[30]

A lifestyle of loving and serving is a little like Christ's sacrificial death on the cross—neither one is convenient; neither one represents the easy route. But what better way is there to get the attention of an increasingly self-oriented world than through acts of selfless service that echo Christ's service on the cross? Such service, naturally expressed and generously offered, is exactly what God permits and encourages and commands us to do, so he may be glorified and his love extended to the whole world. Gene Veith Jr., in his book *God at Work* writes, "In his spiritual Kingdom, we rest in Christ; in his earthly kingdom, we serve our neighbors . . . God expresses his love as he provides for his created order, and he calls human beings into the process."[31]

Whether we serve inside or outside the church, our goal is the same—to glorify God by passing along the love of God that has been so freely given to us. And everywhere we look, both inside and outside the church, we find desperate people in need of service.

Some acts of service God calls us to may be heroic, but most are quite simple. Meals do not cook themselves, lawns do not mow themselves, and clothes do not give themselves away. Babysitters do not appear by magic, and taxis don't take people to church or the grocery store for free. But we can do these things. They are not difficult, and when we do them our lives point to God. "Let your light shine before others, so that they may see your good works and give glory to your Father who is in heaven" (Matthew 5:16).

Remember, though, that we cannot merely go through the motions of love. "God hath many servants," writes Thomas Adams, but very little service in the world."[32] We must know love and feel love for those whom we serve, or our words and actions will ring falsely. As far as the world is concerned, that makes God into a liar and our professed faith into self-righteous moralism. Let's pray that this may not be true in our churches today. May every Christian realize his or her God-given ministry to others. "Do Christ this one favour for all his Love to you," writes Thomas Wilcox, "love all his poor saints and people, the meanest, the weakest, notwithstanding any difference in judgment. They are graven on his Heart . . . Let them be so on yours."[33]

In an essay called "The Love of God," Octavius Winslow included this poem:

I'd carve Your passion on the bark;
And every wounded tree
Shall droop, and bear some mystic mark
That Jesus died for me.
The suitors shall wonder when they read,
Inscribed on all the grove,
That Heaven itself came down and bled,
To win a mortal's love.[34]

"Go forth and BE LOVING," Winslow concludes, "even as your Father in heaven is loving. Let your heart be as large in its creature capacity as God's heart is in its divine."[35]

We engrave people's hearts with God's love by earnestly seeking to love and serve them as Christ has done for us. Such serving will not always be easy, and we will sometimes fail to love our neighbor. But God uses even our mistakes to build his kingdom, because in the end, Christian servanthood is about God's glory, not ours.

If every one of us stepped out in service with affection for each other and for the lost, what then would the world look like?

## Eight
# SUBJECTION

I Can Serve Because I Do Not Belong to Myself

The ocean waves were gentle in the shallows; the water was warm and blue, and the body floating in it was very clearly dead.

Two years earlier, with five ships and 260 men, Ferdinand Magellan had left Spain seeking a western route to the Spice Islands of Asia. A safe return would have proved unequivocally that the Earth was round. It would also have guaranteed Magellan and his family fantastic wealth and power for generations to come. But it all went wrong when the explorer sought to take over the tiny Philippine island of Mactan and was ambushed by natives. Now, his stagnant blood laced with poison from a native dart, Magellan floated lifeless, his dreams of fame and fortune washed up on the shore. As author Laurence Bergreen writes, "His thirst for glory, under the cover of religious zeal, led him fatally astray. In the course of the voyage, Magellan had managed to outwit death many times. In the end, the only peril he could not survive was the greatest of all: himself."[36]

All of us have Dreams of Self. Apart from the direction of God's Spirit, these dreams can come to rule us, often launching us on long voyages of self-glorification. And everyone at some time has seen one of these personal dreams perish in a kind of Mactan Island experience.

What dreams do you hold onto that you haven't submitted to God's will? It doesn't need to involve world domination. It could simply be a need to appear smart, godly, talented, funny, or attractive. It may be a wish for a particular role at church. Whatever it is, all of us are naturally more adept at building our little kingdoms than declaring God's great one. Most of the time, we want to exercise self-rule, not self-control. We want to set sail like Magellan in pursuit of our own glory. Yet Jesus explains that to follow him necessarily means self-denial: "For whoever would save his life will lose it, but whoever loses his life for my sake and the gospel's will save it" (Mark 8:35).

Serving others in pursuit of God's glory rather than our own is perhaps the most effective way we can practice self-denial. Such service reminds us that we do not belong to ourselves — we were purchased at the cross when our Savior and Redeemer paid the price for our sins. In fact, this is what makes true servanthood possible. Empowered by the Holy Spirit, we can serve in the local church *because* we do not belong to ourselves.

So it is not our own will we are called to obey, but God's, so that his agenda might increasingly eclipse our own and become our own. But how do we even begin to do this? Thomas Watson gives a seven-part answer to that question;[37] I want to address three of the seven, which I'm characterizing as follows:

- Self-Controlled: A servant confines himself to one master
- Available: A servant is not independent, but at the disposal of his master
- Satisfied: A servant is satisfied with his master's allowance

## Self-Controlled

<u>A servant confines himself to one master.</u> If we are to be servants who are truly subject to our God, we must maintain a continual effort to leave the service of sin and self, that we might serve God only. This means giving up the Dreams of Self we so dearly cherish and yielding ourselves to another Master. To exercise that kind of self-denial requires self-control.

Self-control is often seen in our culture as simply the suppression of less-noble desires, something that helps us with weight loss, a bad temper, or an addiction. In this view, self-control is essentially a negative thing: "I *will not* do this or that."

In the biblical view, however, self-control has two components, one positive and one negative, with the positive component actually being far more important. Biblical self-control is much more about saying Yes than it is about saying No. It is a saying Yes to God, his commands, and his ways. It is not fundamentally an exercise of personal power for the sake of a personal agenda. It is fundamentally a surrender to God's power for the sake of his agenda — a positive act of reliance on God's strength, so we can live and serve as our Master calls us to.

For the Christian, therefore, self-control involves *obeying* God (a positive act) so that we might get better at *disobeying* our sinful nature (a negative act). If we exercise and eat right simply so we can look better, we merely exchange one self-desire (food and comfort) for a different self-desire (vanity). True self-control is not about exchanging one personal desire for another, but exchanging our desires for God's.

We can do this because, when we come to Christ, God bestows on us a set of spiritual gifts that empower us to live in ways we could not have lived previously (Galatians 5:22-24). These gifts have familiar-sounding names — love, joy, peace, patience, kindness, goodness, faithfulness, gentleness, and ... self-control. You don't need to be a Christian to have some understanding of what these words mean. But when these familiar attributes come to us as spiritual gifts, they take on new power, operating in us and through us in ways that were not possible prior to our salvation.

Peter reveals that the spiritual gift of self-control functions as a step in the sanctification process (2 Peter 1:3-7), sandwiched between knowledge and steadfastness. By growing in our knowledge of Christ and how he has transformed us, we can control our selfish desires. Paul puts it this way: "For the love of Christ controls us, because we have concluded this: that one has died for all, therefore all have died" (2 Corinthians 5:14). That is, knowing what Christ did for us on the cross leads to repentance—a rejection of our values and an embrace of God's.

So, self-control is:

- a spiritual gift;
- that joins with an understanding of the gospel;
- to enable us to refocus our passion from self-will to God's will.

Self-control gives us the power to change masters, as we yield our self-rule so we might become servants of the true King. Through this gift, we can exercise the discipline to focus our service and obedience on one Master.

Jerry Bridges draws an attractive picture of the fruit of self-control: "As we grow in the grace of self control, we will experience the liberation of those who, under the guidance and grace of the Holy Spirit, are freed from the shackles of self-indulgence and are brought into the freedom of true spiritual discipline."[38]

## Available

**A servant is not independent, but at the disposal of his master.** To truly serve God and his agenda, we must be at his disposal regarding whom and how we serve. Biblical service always accomplishes at least two things at the same time: it communicates God's love, and it promotes our ongoing sanctification. To reach those whom God wants to reach, while at the same time helping us grow in holiness, serving will often be inconvenient, distasteful, or both.

Usually there will be something about our call to serve that involves people, places, times, or modes of service for which we feel little desire, or even hostility. But Jesus made no exclusions. He went to places and he served people that were unholy, unfashionable, inconvenient, unattractive, unhealthy, and dangerous. He lost sleep and skipped meals in order to meet needs and speak truth. He did not make exceptions; therefore we cannot, whether our primary calling is to serve inside or outside the church building.

"A servant must not do what he pleases, but be at

the will of his master. Thus, a godly man is a servant. He is wholly at God's disposal,"[39] writes Thomas Boston. Jesus came for the sick, not the healthy; he served the leper and tax collector. Out of Spirit-empowered love for Christ and passion for the gospel, we should be willing to do the same.

My point is not that true serving will always be pure hardship, for there is a unique joy that comes in serving God according to his will. But if we have been serving for some time under conditions that truly suit our comfort and convenience, we are likely serving the master of Self.

## Satisfied

**A servant is satisfied with his master's allowance.**
Most of the things we spend our time on in daily life are closely tied to results, usually in the form of receiving reward or recognition. Working hard in school will earn you good grades. Practicing regularly in sports or music will make you stand out. Applying yourself on the job will get you a raise or promotion. You put something in, you get something out. It's easy to carry over this mentality to service in the church. But biblical servanthood is not about reward, recognition, or even results.

As we seek to serve God wholeheartedly, we will eventually receive reward, in this life or the next (Luke 19:11-27). We may also receive recognition and honor, and there are times when it is right to publicly honor those who serve (Romans 13:7). Finally, we may or may not be able to see any results from our efforts (1 Corinthians 3:5-7). But our *motivation* for serving must not be a desire for any of these things. Our motivation must be to please God and to be satisfied with his allowance and provision. Puritan Jeremiah Burroughs explains in *The Rare Jewel of Christian Contentment*: "But this is the soul's worship, to be subject itself to God . . . I beseech you: in active obedience we worship God by doing what pleases God, but by passive obedience we do as well worship God by being pleased with what God does."[40]

The call to servanthood is a call to worship God by serving others with joy, even when we are not thanked, even if we are mocked, and sometimes even when it seems our service does no actual good. In the absence of recognition, reward, or results, we can be satisfied with what God has done already, what he has promised to do, and whatever he may choose to do in the future. With regard to ourselves, God's ultimate treasure and reward—eternal salvation—has already been given to us through Christ. Can we really ask more of God than this? With regard to those whom we serve, God has promised to make our efforts fruitful in his own time and his own way—one plants, another waters, but God gives the increase.

Do we dare call these rewards insufficient, or these promises too imprecise? In such moments, we either begin to treasure our own glory more than we treasure Christ, or we value our own judgment of what is best above God's judgment. The protection of our authority and role becomes more important to us than the glory of the holy God of the universe. We have stopped magnifying the gospel and begun to magnify ourselves.

Thomas Watson once again explains this so wonderfully: "We glorify God by being contented in that state in which Providence has placed us ...For one to be content when he is in heaven is no wonder; but to be content under the cross is like a Christian."[41]

It comes down to this: Through the spiritual gift of self-control we can exercise the discipline to serve God above ourselves. As servants, not masters, we should be available for service as needed. And, we will leave the outcome of our serving to our Master and Lord. To be in subjection to the will of God, to live in accordance with the fact that he has purchased us for his own purposes, means at least these three things.

# Nine
# **PERSPECTIVE**

Building the Church Eternal


As a young boy, I loved to destroy ant mounds, especially the big one under our orange tree. If a few ants happened to perish in a death ray of refracted sunlight from my dad's magnifying glass, it made me feel like Godzilla. When they swarmed out to repel the Attack of the Giant Sneaker, I felt like a temperamental Greek deity. Yet no matter how often I reduced their world to chaos, the ants were never really defeated. They just rebuilt the same colony, in the same spot, over and over again. It puzzled me. Why would they persist in this obviously futile activity?

For the record, I no longer take joy in decimating ant colonies, and my dad's magnifying glass is safely back with his maps. But sometimes when I think about serving in the church, I actually do remember those ants and how all their efforts just seemed pointless to me. I can be tempted to think that because our world will end when Christ returns, what does it matter if we help build the little anthill of our own local church through serving? There have been millions of Christian churches down through the centuries, each one like a little anthill in its busyness. Many of these have seemingly vanished without a trace, only God really knowing what their ultimate impact has been. Even when the fruitfulness of a particular church is obvious, isn't Christ's work the only thing that produces real results? The whole world is going up in flames anyway, so when all this is wiped out, won't my hard work and sacrifice have been irrelevant?

We can always be tempted to think our service doesn't really matter. Whenever we face this, whenever we are tempted to conclude it's all futile, what we need is the application of a little basic theology.

## The Impact of a Perfect Forever

As you and I look out over the Christian landscape, we see countless local churches, movements, denominations, and organizations that confess Christ but are often deeply divided in matters of doctrine and practice. When God looks out over the Christian landscape, he sees all this, but he also sees the Church, the Bride, the single collection of redeemed individuals who will spend eternity with him. No denomination or movement or local gathering of believers is eternal. But this one great church that God alone can see—comprising all believers past, present, and future—will indeed last forever. Grasping something of the scope of this truth can help us recognize that our service in the local church is anything but futile.

**Our service and our eternity are both grounded in the cross.** We serve because of the cross. Also because of the cross, we can look forward to an eternity with God. Our acts of service are part of a continuum with the cross at the beginning, the church in the middle, and eternity as the never-ending culmination. Serving today is about the cross that is our past and the eternity that is our future.

**Our service celebrates, approximates, and anticipates perfect service, but always does so imperfectly.** As we seek to love and serve one another, we are often painfully aware that our efforts fall short. We live as sinners in a temporary and imperfect world. Here, we cannot love and serve with Christ's perfections, or as well as we will be able to in eternity. Here, nothing is perfect except God and his works. Yet our acts of service and our attempts to love are tied to eternity and its perfections in at least three ways. Our service here *anticipates* our service there. Our service here *approximates* our service there. And our service here

*celebrates*, in advance, the perfect expressions of love
and service that we will perform and experience in
eternity.

**Our service makes a genuine difference,
helping to build all that will one day be perfected.**
Here, by each small act of service, the church is
gradually being unified in the love of Christ. When
Christ returns, we know the church will not yet have
attained perfect unity, because it will still be made
up entirely of sinners. Some kind of transition from
imperfect unity to perfect unity will be necessary.
But there is a specific *point* of unity God desires for
us to reach prior to that day. We dare not conclude
that since God will ultimately perfect everything, we
have no work to do. We remain on earth precisely
*because* there is work to do.

God providentially places us in situations
where we have the opportunity to serve. We are in
our specific communities and relationships by the
mystery of his good will. There is a need you can
fill right where you are, because you are not there
by accident. God lovingly prepares opportunities
for us to exhibit servanthood and participate in
the dispensing of his love and mercy. "For we are
his workmanship, created in Christ Jesus for good
works, which God prepared beforehand, that we
should walk in them" (Ephesians 2:10).

When we leave these bodies we will take up

our eternal occupation as servants and worshipers of God—*this* is the primary reason God takes so seriously our role as servants in this life. He is letting us practice, and giving us a small glimpse of heaven. There, we will be unhindered by mixed motives and sinful desires, free to serve God with all of our hearts, minds, and souls, for all eternity. At the same time, what we do here contributes to what will happen there. Genuine acts of Christian love and service to one another in this life help build a unity within the church that will come to perfection when Christ returns. What we do here really does matter.

## Valuing God's Kingdom

Jesus told us, "The kingdom of heaven is like treasure hidden in a field, which a man found and covered up. Then in his joy he goes and sells all that he has and buys that field" (Matthew 13:44). When we realize the true worth and the radiant brilliance of the kingdom of God, it changes us. We enter this kingdom as individuals, but the fundamental nature of what we enter is corporate. We are called to become citizens of a kingdom ruled by a triune God. What we must recognize is that the best expression of God's kingdom we will ever see on earth is the local church. We are to cherish the local church, with all her imperfections, as if she were treasure in a field.

As we have seen, this kingdom—of which your

local church is an indivisible part—is eternal. The writer of Hebrews encourages us to continue in love and service to one another by pointing to our future inheritance:

> For God is not unjust so as to overlook your work and the love that you have shown for his name in serving the saints, as you still do. And we desire each one of you to show the same earnestness to have the full assurance of hope until the end, so that you may not be sluggish, but imitators of those who through faith and patience inherit the promises.
>
> Hebrews 6:10-12

Once we understand the significance of being part of the eternal kingdom of God, we come to a greater appreciation of the local church. God's Church will never be destroyed, so our service in our local church will never be futile. Paul writes, "The sting of death is sin, and the power of sin is the law. But thanks be to God, who gives us the victory through our Lord Jesus Christ. Therefore, my beloved brothers, be steadfast, immovable, always abounding in the work of the Lord, knowing that in the Lord your labor is not in vain" (1 Corinthians 15:56-58). Paul knew that focusing us on heaven—our ultimate victory over death—would not only

give us fresh strength to serve today. It can cause us
to carry on even when it seems all our efforts to serve
are in vain.

"Go to the ant, O sluggard; consider her ways,
and be wise. Without having any chief, officer, or
ruler, she prepares her bread in summer and gathers
her food in harvest" (Proverbs 6:6-8). Driven by
an instinctive need to survive, ants spend their lives
doing repetitive, menial tasks. In two seconds the
sneaker of a destructive child can destroy weeks
of effort, yet the ants rebuild each time in the same
manner and with the same urgency. We shuffle our
feet and complain because we think serving has no
meaning or eternal significance. When informed by
Scripture, however, we can recognize that serving the
church is of tremendous eternal significance. Serving
now helps to prepare us for heaven later, where we
will serve God around his throne forever. Moreover,
it builds and strengthens the body of Christ on
earth. These eternal truths inform and motivate our
temporal work. All Christians will benefit from the
eternal nature of the church. It is our astonishing
privilege to help build now what God will perfect
and sustain forever.

You and I may not be serving in the role or under
the circumstances we consider ideal. But God is
after something bigger than our preferences. The
picture here is so much larger than our limited view

of what seems best. God is building his church, and he is doing it one act of service, one soul, and one congregation at a time, in hundreds of cultures, over centuries and millennia.

In all our love and service we must look back to the cross for inspiration and purpose, and look forward to eternity with God where all our efforts will be redeemed, and all our weak attempts will be made strong. Serving in the local church is a small reflection of what our future in heaven will be like. God has planned our works of service from eternity past so that they will affect eternity future. So let us take joy in the fact that we are practicing for eternity, attempting to mimic as best we can what will take place when all of God's purposes for this world have been accomplished. All imperfect service here will be perfected there, as an untold number of redeemed souls are fully unified together in Christ.

It is absolutely amazing what a little serving will do.

# APPENDICES

## A Comment on Sanctification

Turning away from sin and toward God is a lifelong pursuit, a process called sanctification by which we become more like the image of Christ. Justification—our position before God—is solely a work of God, but sanctification requires our active participation. Wayne Grudem defines sanctification as "a progressive work of God and man that makes us more and more free from sin and like Christ in our actual lives." The sanctification process begins when we are saved and continues as long as we are in this body.

When Christians speak of the fight against sin or our desire to serve God, we often use the language of absolutes: "yielding everything to God," or "turning away from sin completely." Such language can seem to suggest that a life of perfect sinlessness is possible while still in these bodies. Indeed, we use some of that language in this book. Why? Because it helps us be serious about our dedication to God. It keeps truth right there on the table. It reminds us there are no greater issues in this life than those involving sin and holiness. It helps us exercise vigilance in a battle that genuinely matters.

But as we use this language of absolutes, let us not lose sight of the fact that our battle is ongoing, and let us maintain a holy fear of this truth: at each moment, we are still terribly capable of sin.

# A Brief History of Service in the Church

The events of November 9, 1989 will always remain a vivid and cherished memory of mine. The Berlin Wall was opened. For forty years, Eastern Germany had lived under Soviet political, economic, and military control. With the Iron Curtain torn apart, families and friends and an entire country were reunited in political and economic freedom. East Germans were once again free to travel, work, live, and vote in whatever manner they desired without the fear of imprisonment or punishment.

As influential as this event was, another day on which an entirely different barrier was broken stands out as the most glorious and memorable day of human history. Some two thousand years ago, a temple curtain made of "blue and purple and crimson fabrics and fine linen" tore from top to bottom (2 Chronicles 3:14). The tearing of this curtain altered the very nature of the relationship between God and man.

The curtain that separated the Most Holy Place from the rest of the Jewish temple was both like and unlike every other curtain before or since. For most curtains, it is not the materials they are made from, but the things they separate that define their importance. Unlike all other curtains in history, however, the holy veil was vastly more significant because of whom it separated. It represented the inaccessibility and infinite separation between God and his creation under the Old Covenant. But why did God need separation from his own creation (Genesis 1:27), especially those created in his own image?

God designed and designated the Most Holy Place as his "footstool" on Earth, where priests made sacrifices atoning for the sins of Israel. The room served as a way for Israel to approach God, but due to the sins committed against him, it was all but inaccessible (1 Chronicles 6:49). By this system, God could "dwell among the people of Israel and . . . be their

God" (Exodus 29:45-46). Thus, the curtain symbolized that man could not freely fellowship with God directly.

Such stark separation was not always the case. The first man, Adam, was created in God's image—not just in form, but also in purity. Thomas Boston writes, "In this sense, man was made upright (agreeable to the nature of God, whose work is perfect), without any imperfection, corruption, or principle of corruption, in his body or soul. He was made "upright," that is, straight with the will and law of God, without any irregularity in his soul."[42] There was no sin in Adam and consequently he enjoyed perfect fellowship with God.

The first thing God apparently said to Adam besides Be fruitful and multiply was a call to serve, when "the Lord God took the man and put him in the Garden of Eden to work it and keep it" (Genesis 2:15). Notice the command to serve is given before sin enters the world. The command to service was not a result of the Fall. It was a righteous blessing bestowed on man by God. God initiated a relationship with Adam by allowing and instructing him to watch over God's perfect creation, Earth. Adam was to apply his gifts and all his devotion to the task God had given him.

God created humankind to serve and worship in God's first temple—the Garden of Eden. God gave man rulership over the earth and direct access to the Father. This was servanthood in its purest form. There was no bitterness, no hardship—just perfect joy and communion with God. God gave Adam and his wife Eve everything they needed. The only restriction God placed on them was not to eat of the tree of knowledge of good and evil (Genesis 2:17).

When Adam eventually ate the forbidden fruit, his sin created a separation between humankind and God. Consequently, Adam's communion with and service to God were dramatically altered. Adam and Eve were cast out of the Garden, and their work now became fraught with hardship (Genesis 3:17-23). Thus, Adam, having been removed from God's temple on earth (i.e. the Garden of Eden), could no

longer serve in direct communion with God. Adam's sin placed
a barrier between himself and God, and so in turn the nature
of Adam's service changed from steward to outcast.

### How the Fall Affected Servanthood
The backdrop of man's sin against a Holy God provides the context
for serving in the Old Testament. In the Old Testament book of
Exodus, God tells Moses and Aaron to advise Pharaoh eight
different times to "Let my people go, that they may serve me" — *not*
that they may be freed from persecution. Later in Exodus, as
Moses leads them through the desert, God institutes a series of
commandments for the Israelites to keep.

The First Commandment God gives the Jews is to serve him
exclusively (Exodus 20:4-6). This was no coincidence. Israel was
to serve no one or nothing else besides the one true God. It is also
the only commandment for which there are both blessings and
penalties—to the third and fourth generations, no less.

In the first five books of the Bible, God continually and
specifically directs how the Israelites were to serve him
(Deuteronomy 6:13). In some points, the details of how Israel should
serve God are so precise and unyielding that it seems monotonous
today, including chapter upon chapter delineating who can serve
in the temple. Jobs within the temple were exclusively bestowed
to the families of Aaron and his son Levi—no one from any another
tribe was allowed to serve.

God not only prescribed which family would perform which
duty, he also provided exacting details for every job. God lays out
the order of comprehensive rituals, the precise measurements,
and the specific materials that are to be used in the building
of the Temple (Leviticus 19:5-7). Why would God care about
seemingly tedious minutia? Throughout all the details, God was
communicating how serious serving was. He wanted the Israelites
to see that serving in the temple was so important that utter
precision was a necessity.

Service in the temple was so serious that it had to be done in
certain ways, or the deviant risked excommunication by both God

and his people. For example, the book of Leviticus 19:8 states, "And everyone who eats [unclean sacrificial meat] shall bear his iniquity, because he has profaned what is holy to the Lord, and that person shall be cut off from his people."The priests had to perform atoning rituals with exact timing and precision or else incur the wrath of God.

If done the wrong way or by the wrong person, serving in theTemple was a dangerous affair. In Numbers 18:7, God warns Aaron that anyone approaching the altar in the temple who was not qualified for priesthood would die: "And you and your sons with you shall guard your priesthood for all that concerns the altar and that is within the veil; and you shall serve. I give your priesthood as a gift, and any outsider who comes near shall be put to death." Through such seemingly harsh penalties, God communicates how serious our sin is—that it deserves death. Consequently, Israel had to serve God in such way so as to avoid bringing sin into his presence. Serving in the temple was serious to God, because his holiness was at stake.

### Serving in the New Covenant

Jesus hung on the cross after a lifetime of perfect obedience and perfect love for God. He endured the wrath of God as payment for our sins, so that we may be cleansed of guilt and be found acceptable before God (Ephesians 2: 13-16). As Christ died on the cross, the curtain separating the Most Holy Place was torn asunder (Matthew 27:50-52). This destruction of the curtain did not happen arbitrarily or randomly. It was a correlated and subsequent result of the death of Jesus Christ, the Son of God who humbled himself by taking the form of a man and becoming the acceptable sacrifice for man's sin.

After Jesus Christ paid our penalty, he died while still nailed to the Cross. It was at this moment—not before—that the temple curtain was torn. Immediately (and significantly) upon Christ's death, God removed his presence from the temple and signified the alteration in humankind's access to him.The book of Hebrews explains, "But when Christ appeared as a high priest of the good things that have come, then through the greater and more perfect tent (not made with hands, that is, not of this creation) he entered once for all into the holy places, not by means of the blood of goats and calves but by means of his own blood, thus securing an eternal redemption" (Hebrews 9:11-12).

G.K. Beale writes, "Thus, the rending of the veil indicates both a cosmic and cultic reality: the inbreaking destruction of the old creation and the inauguration of the new creation, which introduces access for all believers to God's holy presence in a way that was not available in the old creation."[43]

This new access to God through Christ does not alter God's serious nature towards service. Instead, it sends out to every Christian the call to serve in the church (Hebrews 10). All believers are free to serve, because Christ abolished all of the regulations surrounding service in the church. Each of us now has the privilege and pleasure of serving in the presence of God.

Thus, when the temple curtain was supernaturally slit in two, it represented more than just the power of God to rip drapery. It signified that the temple in Jerusalem was no longer the main access point to God's unique presence on earth. Instead, through the outpouring of the Holy Spirit, God granted personal and unlimited accessibility of his presence to all of those who placed their faith in Christ (Hebrews 10:19-24).

God literally blew the doors off the temple, declaring it obsolete. In place of a temple made of stone, God beckoned humanity to become living temples through faith in Jesus Christ. He promised to place his Spirit in these new, living temples and through them magnify his glory on earth. Paul states in 1 Corinthians 3:16, "Do you not know that you are God's temple and that God's Spirit dwells in you." Inherent to this new bond is a radical shift in how we as living temples can serve in the presence of God. "For if the blood of goats and bulls, and the sprinkling of defiled persons with the ashes of a heifer, sanctify for the purification of the flesh, how much more will the blood of Christ, who through the eternal Spirit offered himself without blemish to God, purify our conscience from dead works to serve the living God" (Hebrews 9:13-14).

The pleasure, honor, and responsibility of serving the church is now extended to all those who have placed their faith in Jesus Christ for salvation. Serving in the presence of God is no longer confined to a set group of people, nor to a small temple room; through the work of Christ, the throne of Grace is accessible for everyone. God's presence in the person of the Holy Spirit now resides in every one of his people. G.K Beale writes, "The Spirit's gifts, formerly limited to prophets, kings and priests, usually for service in connection with the temple, are universalized to all God's people from every race, young and old, male and female."[44]

Every Christian has become a recipient of the Holy Spirit, thereby transforming into a living, breathing temple, and can boldly approach God without fear of personal uncleanness or messing up detailed rituals. In the Old Covenant, serving was a complex and deadly proposition. In the New Covenant, serving is a response to Christ himself. God no longer needs to establish complex rituals and erect barriers between himself and his people, for God now through his Spirit resides in all believers, making them a temple in and of themselves. Every Christian can now serve in the church without fear of death, because Christ has made a way for sinful man to be in fellowship with God. By tearing the symbolic curtain, God has initiated a new era of ministry—the ministry of all believers.

# NOTES

1. Paul David Tripp, *A Quest for More* (New Growth Press, 2007) p 49

2. Leadership Network, *Church Planting Overview*, p 3

3. Mars Hill, Mars Hill Annual Report 2009, p 12

4. John Stott, *The Message of Ephesians* (InterVarsity Press, 1991) p 168

5. Thomas Watson, *A Body of Modern Divinity* (Banner of Truth, 1983) p 205

6. John Calvin, *Institutes of the Christian Religion Vol. 1* (Westminster John Knox Press, 2006) 2.16.15

7. Westminster Shorter Catechism, Q24-26

8. Louis Berkhof, *Systematic Theology* (William B. Eerdmans Publishing, 1938) 403

9. www.baseballhalloffame.org

10. Edmund Clowney, *The Church* (IVP Academic, 1995) p 117

11. ibid, p. 81

12. Thomas Watson, *A Body of Divinity* (Benedection Classics, 2010) p 8

13. Ibid.

14. John Stott, Christ the Controversialist (InterVarsity Press, 1996) pp 162-163

15. J.I Packer, *Knowing God* (IVP Connect, 1993) p 37

16. John Calvin, Institutes 1.1.1

17. Berkhof, *Systematic Theology,* p 247

18. Ralph Venning, *The Sinfulness of Sin* (Banner of Truth, 1996) p 30

19. John Murray, Redemption Accomplished and Applied (Eerdmans, 1954) p 117

20. Martin Luther, *Concerning Christian Liberty* (Kessinger, 2004)

21. C.J. Mahaney, *Christ Our Mediator* (Multnomah, 2004) p 93

22. Martin Luther, *Concerning Christian Liberty*. p 29

23. Gene Veith Jr., *God at Work* (CrosswayBooks, 2002) p 42

24. www.Vegansociety.com

25. Octavius Winslow, *The Love of God*, 1870

26. Westminster Shorter Catechism Q6

27. John Stott, *The Cross of Christ* (IVP Books, 2006) p 249

28. Clowney, *The Church* pg. 79

29. James M. Boice, Foundations of the Christian Faith (IVP Academic, 1986) p 502

30. Paul David Tripp, *Broken-Down House* (Shepherd Press, 2009) p 143

31. Gene Veith Jr., *God at Work* (CrosswayBooks, 2002) pp 38-42

32. I.D.E Thomas, *A Puritan Golden Treasury*, p 258

33. Thomas Wilcox *Honey Out of The Rock* (Chapel Library, 2000) p 28

34. Winslow, *The Love of God*

35. ibid

36. Laurence Bergreen, *Over the Edge of the World* (Harper Perennial, 2004) p 284

37. Thomas Watson, *The Godly Man's Picture* (Banner of Truth, 1992) pp 36-38

38. Jerry Bridges, *The Practice of Godliness* (NavPress 1996) p 144

39. Thomas Boston, *Human Nature In Its Fourfold State*

40. Jeremiah Burroughs, *The Rare Jewel of Christian Contentment (Sovereign Grace Publishers, 2001)* p 120

41. Thomas Watson, *A Body of Divinity* (Benediction Classics, 2010) p 13

42. Thomas Boston, *Human Nature In Its Fourfold State*, p 38

43. G.K Beale, *The Temple and the Church's Mission* (IVP Academinc, 2004) p 190

44. Beale, *The Temple and the Church's Mission* pp 209-210

**CruciformPress.com**

Published by Cruciform Press, Adelphi, Maryland | info@CruciformPress.com | Copyright © 2010 by Nathan Palmer, All rights reserved. | ISBN: 978-1-4538187-7-0 | Unless otherwise indicated, all Scripture quotations are taken from: The Holy Bible: English Standard Version, Copyright © 2001 by Crossway Bibles, a division of Good News Publishers. Used by permission. All rights reserved. | Italics or bold text within Scripture quotations indicate emphasis added.

# ABOUT CRUCIFORM PRESS

**What would a book-publishing company for gospel-centered Christians look like if it began with the realities of 21st century technology?**

We think It would focus on Content, Simplicity, Reliability, Trust, Convenience, Voice, and Community. Here's what we mean by that. These are our promises to you.

**Content:** Every book will be helpful, inspiring, biblical, and gospel-focused.

**Simplicity:** Every book will be short, clear, well-written, well-edited, and accessible.

**Reliability:** A new book will be released the first day of each month. Every book will be the same price. Each book will have a unique cover, yet all our books will maintain a distinctive, recognizable look.

**Trust:** If you like this book, then you're probably a lot like us in how you think, what you believe. and how you see the world. That means you can trust us to give you only the good stuff.

**Convenience:** Our books will be available in print, in a variety of ebook formats, and as audiobooks. Print or ebook subcription opportunities can save you time and money.

**Voice:** We want to know what you'd like to read about, or who you think we ought to consider as an author, or really anything constructive you'd care to say about what we're doing and how we're doing it.

**Community:** We want to encourage and facilitate the sense of community that naturally exists among Christians who love the gospel of grace.

**JOIN US.** Sign up for our newsletter at **CruciformPress.com**

WRESTLING with AN ANGEL

A Story of Love, Disability and the Lessons of Grace

Greg Lucas

CrosswayPress

"C.S. Lewis wrote that he paradoxically loved *The Lord of the Rings* because it 'broke his heart'—and Greg Lucas' writing does the same for me. "
**Justin Taylor**
**Managing Editor**
**ESV Study Bible**

"Witty... stunning... striking... humorous and heartfelt. In our culture which is so quick to devalue life, *Wrestling with an Angel* provides a fresh, honest look at one father's struggle to embrace God in the midst of his son's disability. Can sheer laughter and weeping gracefully coexist in a world of so much affliction? Greg knows all about it. And inside these pages he passes on his lessons of grace to us. I highly recommend this wonderfully personal book!"
**Joni Eareckson Tada**
**Joni and Friends International Disability Center**

"It is the rare book that makes much of God and our dependency on Him while also celebrating His goodness through hard things. This book is a gift to the church, and particularly to men who need an example of masculine, biblical leadership in the face of complex, confusing, and overwhelming circumstances."
**John Knight**
**Senior Director for Development, Desiring God**

"You will laugh; you will cry. You will feel sick; you will feel inspired. You will be repulsed by the ugliness of sin; you will be overwhelmed by the love of God. Greg Lucas takes us on an unforgettable ride as he extracts the most beautiful insights into grace from the most painful experiences of life."

**David P. Murray**
**Puritan Reformed Theological Seminary**

"This is not primarily a book for parents of special-needs children. There is only one disability that keeps a person from heaven, the sin that lives in our hearts. Greg Lucas is a captivating storyteller. When he writes about life with Jake, I recognize God's grace and loving persistence in my life. I want more!

**Noël Piper**
**Author, and wife of pastor and author John Piper**

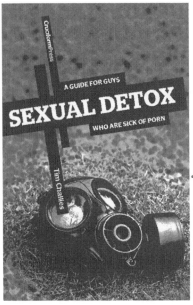

"In an age when sex is worshiped as a god, a little book like this can go a long way to helping men overcome sexual addiction."

**Pastor Mark Driscoll**
**Mars Hill Church**

"Online pornography is not just a problem for Christian men; it is THE problem. Many men, young and old, in our churches need *Sexual Detox*. Challies o ers practical, doable and, above all, gospel-centered hope for men. I want every man I serve and all the guys on our sta  to read this book."
**Tedd Tripp**
**Pastor, and author of Shepherding a Child's Heart**

"Tim Challies strikes just the right balance in this necessary work. His assessment of the sexual epidemic in our culture is sober but not without hope. His advice is practical but avoids a checklist mentality. His discussion of sexual sin is frank without being inappropriate. This book will be a valuable resource."
**Kevin DeYoung**
**Pastor and author**

"Thank God for using Tim to articulate simply and unasham-
edly the truth about sex amidst a culture of permissiveness.
Read it and believe it."

**Ben Zobrist,**
**Tampa Bay Rays**

"Sexual Detox is just what we need. It is clear, honest, and
biblical, written with a tone that is knowing but kind, exhor-
tative but gracious, realistic but determined. We have been
given by Tim Challies a terri c resource for ghting sin and
exalting Christ."

**Owen Strachan**
**Boyce College**

"Tim Challies is one of the nest young evangelical thinkers
of our day."

**Al Mohler**
**President, Southern Baptist Theological Seminary**

"I don't know of a more reliable or more proli c commentator
on the contemporary evangelical scene."

**John MacArthur**
**Pastor-Teacher, Grace Community Church**

# RECLAIMING ADOPTION: MISSIONAL LIVING THROUGH REDISCOVERY OF ABBA FATHER

## DAN CRUVER, EDITOR

## JOHN PIPER
## RICK PHILLIPS
## SCOTTY SMITH
## JASON KOVACS

## AVAILABLE JANUARY 1, 2011

# WE RELEASE A NEW BOOK THE FIRST DAY OF EACH MONTH

# SHORT. CLEAR. CONCISE. HELPFUL. INSPIRING. RELIABLE. GOSPEL-FOCUSED.

# SUBSCRIPTIONS
# $6.49 PRINT
# $3.99 EBOOK

# JOIN US!